BEASTLY BUGS

First published in 2015
This edition published in 2021 by Kingfisher
an imprint of Macmillan Children's Books
The Smithson, 6 Briset Street, London, EC1M 5NR
Associated companies throughout the world
www.panmacmillan.com

Series editor: Sarah Snashall
Series design: Little Red Ant and Laura Hall
Illustrations: Laura Hall
Adapted from an original text by Anita Ganeri and Thea Feldman

ISBN 978-0-7534-4635-5

9 8 7 6 5 4 3 2 1

1TR/1120/WKT/UG/105MA

A CIP catalogue record for this book is available from the British Library.

Printed in China

Picture credits
The Publisher would like to thank the following for permission to reproduce their material.
Top = t; Bottom = b; Centre = c; Left = l; Right = r
Cover Shutterstock/Serg64; Back cover Shutterstock/Vishnevskiy Vasily; Pages 2–3, 4t, 30–31 Shutterstock/QiuJu Song; 4–5 Shutterstock/Kreatif Multimedia; 4l Shutterstock/Henrik Larsson; 4r Shutterstock/Dionisvera; 5tl Shutterstock/HandmadePictures; 5bl Shutterstock/alslutsky; 5tr Shutterstock/kamnuan; 5cr Shutterstock/grafvision; 5br Shutterstock/Vishnevskiy Vasily; 6 Shutterstock/artjazz; 6l Shutterstock/PHOTO FUN; 7 Naturepl/Stephen Dalton; 8 Shutterstock/Allocricetulus; 9 Shutterstock/Eric Isselee; 10 Flickr/Gilles San Martin; 11t Shutterstock/Bildagentur Zoonar GmbH; 11b Ardea/John Clegg; 12 Shutterstock/Vasily Vishnevskiy; 13 Shutterstock/Michael Warwick; 14 Shutterstock/orionmystery; 15t Shutterstock/Cathy Keifer; 15 Flickr/Joshua Byrd; 15b Kingfisher Artbank; 16 Shutterstock/Dimijana; 16t Shutterstock/pan demin; 17 Shutterstock/Evgeniy Ayupov; 18–19 Kingfisher Artbank; 19t Shutterstock/ M Dykstra; 19b Shutterstock/Cathy Keifer; 20 Naturepl/Kim Taylor; 21 Shutterstock/orionmystery; 22t Kingfisher Artbank; 22b Naturepl/Hans Christoph Kappel; 23 Shutterstock/Anton Harder; 24 Shutterstock/Cathy Keifer; 25 FLPA/Erica Olsen; 25b Shutterstock/Wasan Ritthawon; 26 Shutterstock/reptiles4all; 27t Shutterstock/Tatsiana_S; 27b Shutterstock/Platsee; 28–29 Shutterstock/cyrrpit; 31b Shutterstock/M Dykstra; 32 Shutterstock/Evgeniy Ayupov.

For your free audio download go to

http://panmacmillan.com/BeastlyBugs

or goo.gl/nw2dJO

Happy listening!

Scan me!

CONTENTS

It's a bug world! 4

Bugs all around 6

Insect or spider? 8

Bugs on the move 10

The amazing monarch 12

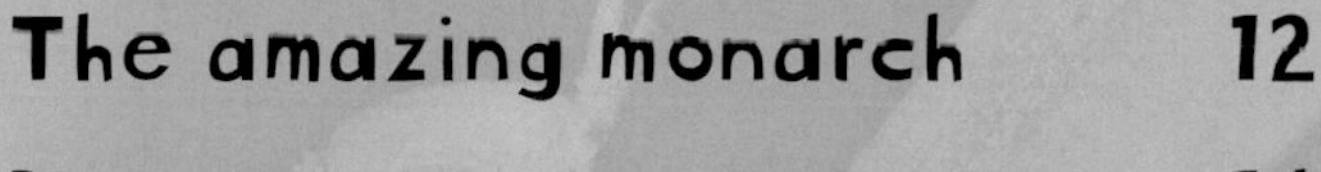

Bug senses 14

Lunchtime 16

Butterfly life story 18

Good mothers 20

Bug builders 22

Fangs and stings 24

Hide and seek 26

Hairy monster 28

Glossary 30

Index 32

It's a bug world!

There is a whole mini-world of tiny bugs all around us. There are insects such as ants, wasps, butterflies and beetles, and other minibeasts such as spiders, slugs, snails, woodlice, leeches and centipedes.

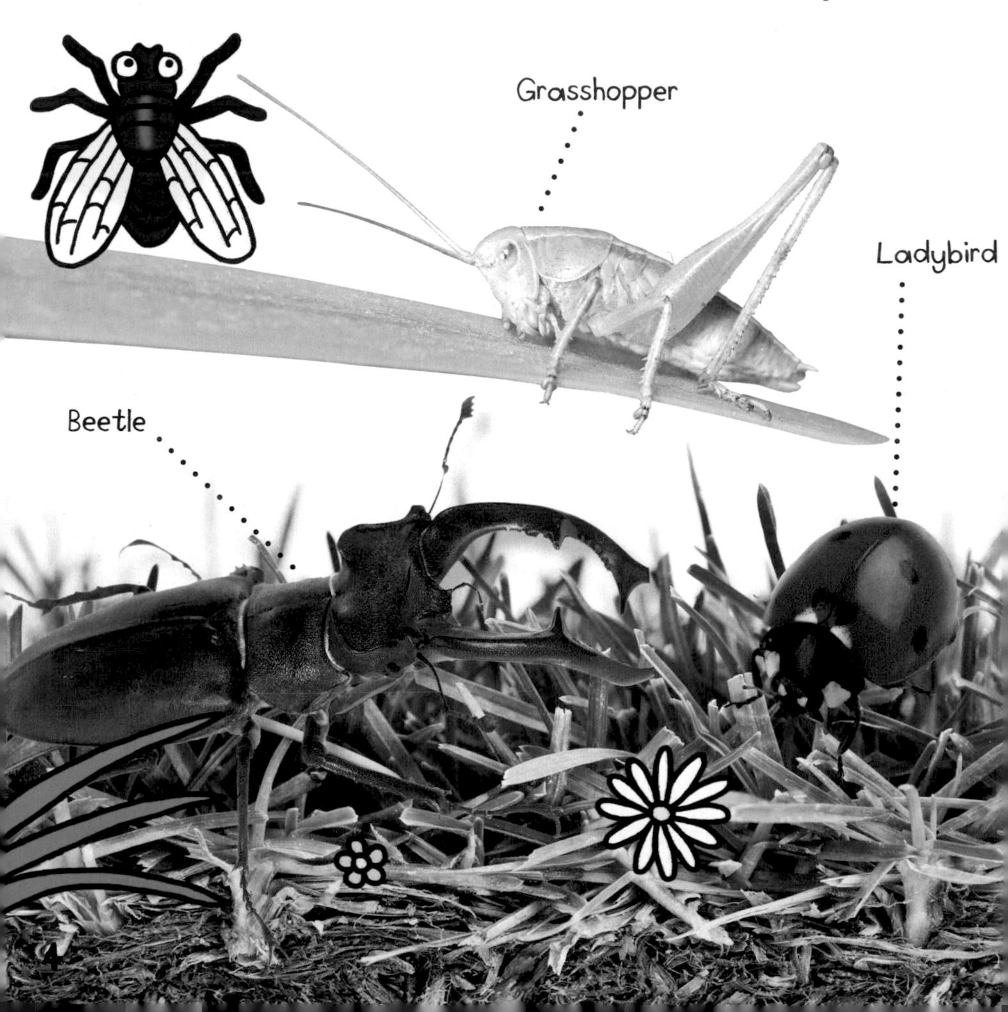

Most minibeasts live on land, but some live in freshwater such as ponds and rivers.

Millipede

FACT ...

There are millions of insect species. That's more than any other kind of animal!

Bugs all around

Bugs and minibeasts live almost everywhere: in fields, woods, rivers and towns. Watch butterflies feeding on flowers. Turn over a stone to find a woodlouse. Look out for webs outside and you'll know there are spiders living nearby.

Earthworms live underground.

SPOTLIGHT: Diving bell spider

Record breaker:	lives underwater
Size:	up to 15mm
Lives:	Europe and northern Asia
Eats:	tiny fish and larvae

Insect or spider?

Every insect has six legs and a three-part body. Most insects have wings and can fly.

FACT ...

A honeybee flaps its wings about 250 times a second to stay in the air.

A spider has eight legs and a two-part body. Most spiders have eight eyes. Spiders do not have wings.

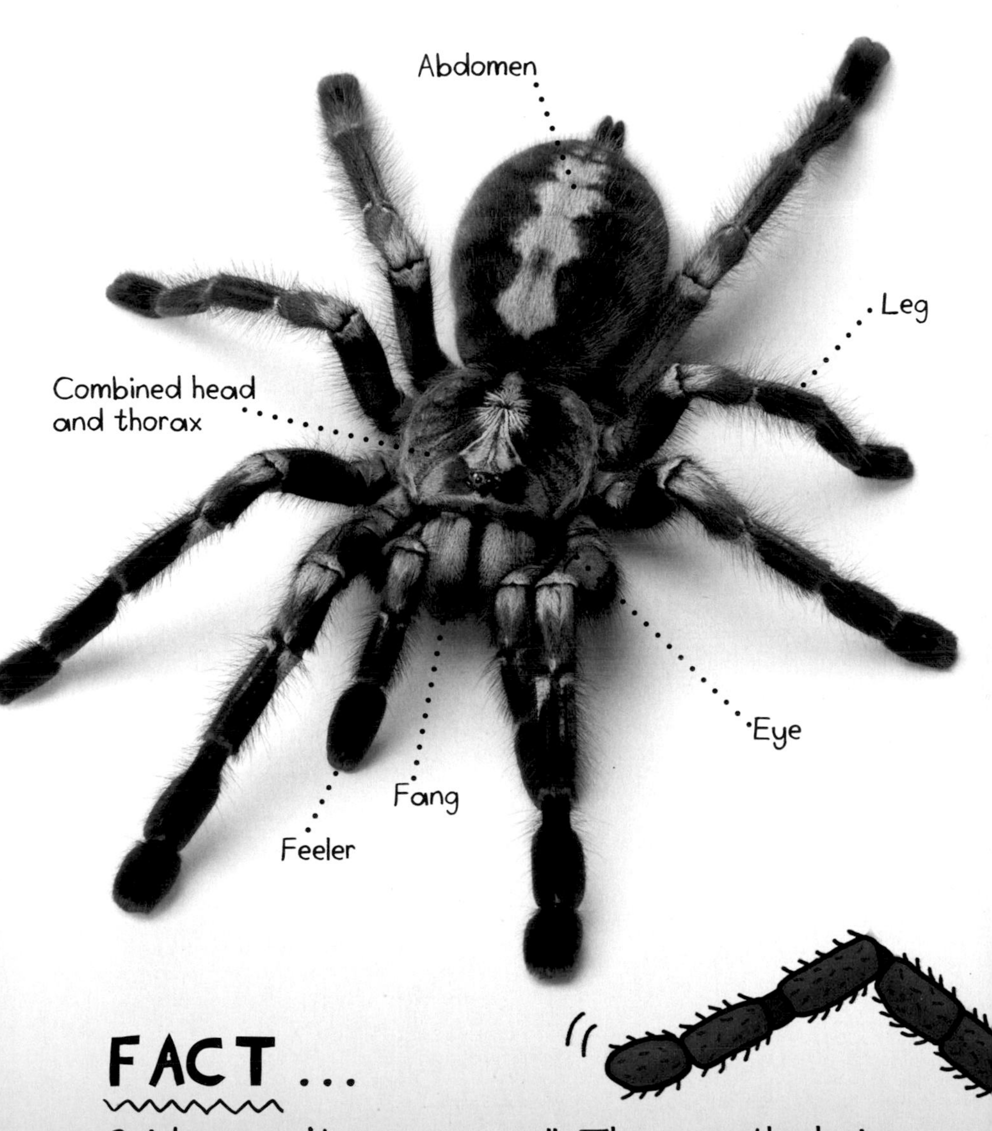

FACT ...

Spiders can't see very well. They use the hairs on their body to help them find their way.

Bugs on the move

Minibeasts move in different ways. Grasshoppers, froghoppers, fleas and crickets hop. Slugs and snails slide. Spiders, ants and cockroaches crawl. Grasshoppers, dragonflies, butterflies and beetles fly.

FACT ...

Some millipedes have 375 pairs of legs – that's 750 legs altogether!

A grasshopper can jump and fly.

FACT ...

Slugs and snails make a slimy track and then slide along it.

SPOTLIGHT: Froghopper

Record breaker:	highest jumper for its size
Size:	up to 7mm
Lives:	worldwide
Eats:	plant sap

A water boatman uses its legs to row across the water.

The amazing monarch

Some minibeasts don't travel very far: they crawl up a plant stem, or fly from tree to tree. This is not the case for monarch butterflies.

In the autumn these butterflies fly 3000 kilometres from Canada to the warm weather in California, USA, or Mexico. In the spring they return to Canada.

Every year millions of globe-skimmer dragonflies glide from India to Africa.

FACT ...

Monarch butterflies fly to the same place every year. Sometimes they even find the same trees.

Bug senses

Insects have clever eyes that are very good at seeing movement. Each eye has hundreds of lenses and each one is like a tiny eye. Insects also have antennae to smell, taste and touch things.

FACT ...

A cricket has ears on its front legs.

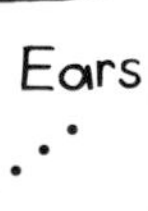

This male moth has long antennae that look like feathers.

Spotlight: Dragonfly

Record breaker:	most lenses (30,000) per eye
Size:	wingspan up to 120mm
Lives:	worldwide
Eats:	small insects

Lunchtime

Many minibeasts eat plants, but some eat meat, blood and each other!

Bees visit flowers to drink nectar and to collect pollen for their young.

A leech sticks onto an animal with its sucker, then starts to drink.

Gardeners love ladybirds because they eat aphids and other pests.

FACT ...

Cockroaches aren't fussy eaters. They eat almost anything, from plants to the rubbish you throw in the bin.

This mantis is eating a spider.

Butterfly life story

Here is the story of how a tiny egg becomes a beautiful butterfly.

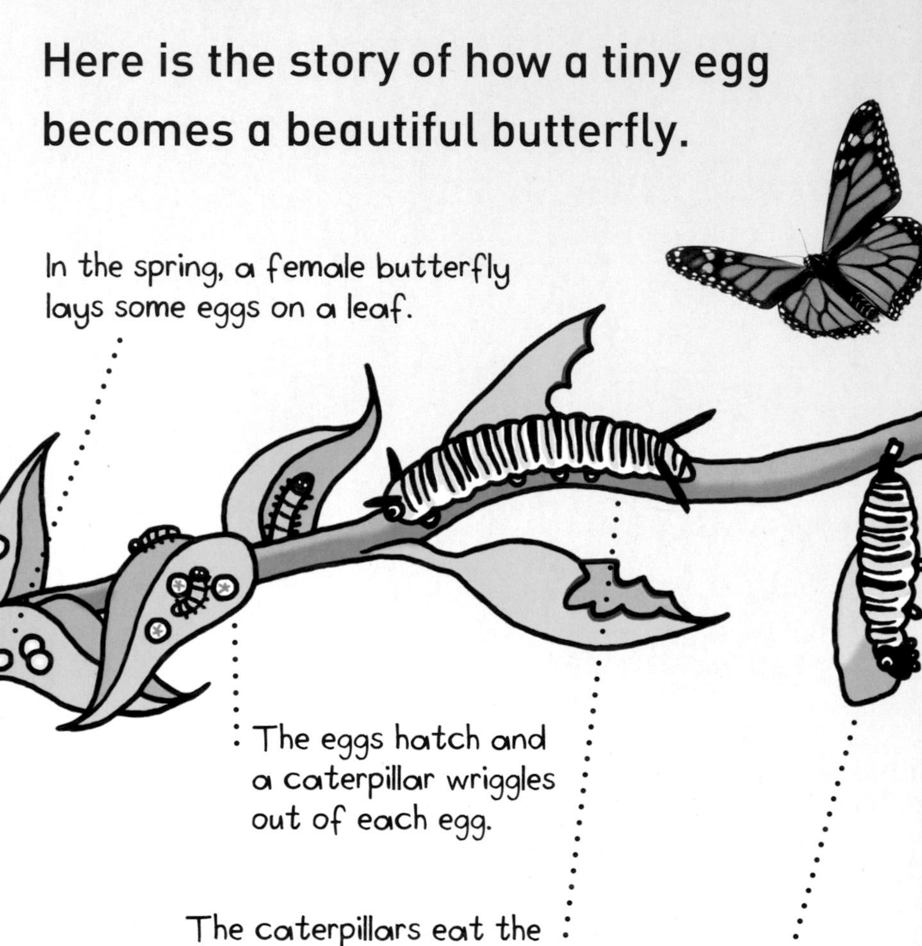

FACT...

A female butterfly can lay 100 eggs every day!

Inside the case, the caterpillar's body turns into a butterfly.

The chrysalis splits open and the butterfly wriggles out. When its wings have dried in the Sun, it flies away.

A butterfly's wings are soft and wet when it comes out of the chrysalis. It waits for the Sun to dry them.

Good mothers

Most minibeasts lay eggs then leave them, but there are a few who look after their eggs.

A mother earwig lays her eggs in a hole in the ground. She keeps them clean and protects them.

Female earwig protecting her eggs

A female wolf spider carries her eggs on her back inside a ball of silk. When the baby spiders hatch, they climb onto their mother's back.

Female wolf spider and spiderlings

FACT ...

A cuckoo bee doesn't look after her eggs. She lays them in the nest of another bee.

Bug builders

Some minibeasts build nests where they lay their eggs. Others build webs and traps to catch food.

Honeybees build a hive in a hole in a tree.

A trapdoor spider waits for its prey in a burrow with a trap door.

SPOTLIGHT: Spinifex termite

Record breaker:	builds tallest nests
Size:	5mm
Lives:	Australia
Eats:	woody part of plants

FACT ...

Termites build enormous mud nests. Some termite towers are three times higher than a tall person.

Fangs and stings

Some spiders and insects use venom to kill their prey or to protect themselves.

A spider pierces its prey's skin with its fangs and injects venom.

Spotlight: European hornet

Record breaker:	largest European wasp
Size:	up to 35mm
Lives:	worldwide
Eats:	wasps, large moths, bees

If a wasp is attacked, it can inject venom into its attacker through a long, sharp sting.

Bombardier beetle ready to attack

A bombardier beetle shoots a jet of hot poison at its enemies. It fires the venom out of its tail. Bang!

Hide and seek

Many bugs use colour and pattern to hide from attackers or from their prey. If a small insect lands on this flower, it gets a nasty shock. A mantis is camouflaged on the flower!

Can you spot the mantis?

FACT ...

A hawk-moth has eyes on its wings. They're not real eyes but they look scary to birds.

The leaf insect is the same colour as the leaf it lives on.

Hairy monster

Some minibeasts are not mini at all. The Goliath bird-eating tarantula is the biggest spider in the world. It lives in a burrow and comes out at night to look for food.

The Goliath bird-eating tarantula eats insects, other spiders, lizards and birds. It waits for them to come near, then attacks.

SPOTLIGHT: Goliath bird-eating tarantula

Record breaker:	world's largest spider
Size:	25cm
Lives:	South America
Eats:	insects, rodents, frogs

FACT ...

If a bird-eating spider is scared, it hisses and flicks hairs into its attacker's face.

GLOSSARY

abdomen The back part of an insect's body.

antennae Long thin parts on an insect's head. They are used for smelling, tasting and touching.

aphid A tiny insect that eats plants.

burrow A hole that an animal digs in the ground to live or lay its eggs in.

centipede A long minibeast with lots of body sections and lots of legs.

chrysalis The hard case that a caterpillar makes around its body.

fang A tooth that squirts poison as it bites.

glide To move through the air without flapping the wings.

hive A nest built by bees.

insect A minibeast with six legs and a hard case around its body.

leech A minibeast that drinks the blood of other animals.

lens Clear round parts in an animal's eyes that help it to see.

nectar A sweet liquid inside flowers that many insects drink.

pollen A powder made inside flowers that helps to make seeds.

termite A tiny creature that builds huge tower-like nests.

thorax The middle part of an insect's body, between the head and the abdomen.

venom A kind of poison that some spiders and snakes make inside their body. They use it to harm or kill other animals.

INDEX

antenna 14, 15

bees 5, 8, 16, 21, 22
beetles 4, 7, 10, 25
butterflies 4, 5, 6, 10, 12–13, 18–19

caterpillars 18–19
centipedes 4
cockroaches 10, 17
crickets 10, 14

dragonflies 10, 12, 15

earthworms 6
earwigs 20
eyes 8, 9, 14, 15, 27

fangs 9, 24

grasshoppers 4, 10, 24

leeches 4, 16

mantises 17, 26
millipedes 5, 10
moths 15, 27

nests 21, 22, 23, 25

poison 24, 25

slugs 4, 5, 10, 11
snails 4, 7, 10, 11
spiders 4, 5, 6, 7, 9, 10, 15, 17, 21, 22, 24, 28, 29

tarantula 28–29
termites 23

venom 24, 25

wasps 4, 25
water boatmen 11
wings 8, 9, 15, 19, 27